Sacred Prayers and chants: Prathana

A collection of bhajans, kirtan, chalisas, aartee and mantras for Hindu religious ceremonies.

Preface:

Namaste, welcome to this sacred compilation of prayers from the rich tapestry of Hindu tradition. Within these pages, you will discover a treasure trove of verses, mantras, and invocations that have been cherished for millennia by seekers and devotees around the world. Hinduism, with its profound depth and diversity, offers a multitude of pathways to connect with the divine. In this prayer book, we have endeavoured to capture a glimpse of that vastness, selecting prayers that resonate with the soul and inspire the heart to soar in devotion. Whether you are embarking on a journey of self-discovery, seeking solace in times of trial, or simply yearning to deepen your connection with the divine, these prayers offer a sanctuary for the spirit. They are a testament to the enduring wisdom of our ancient sages and the eternal truths that underpin the universe.

As you immerse yourself in these sacred words, may you feel the presence of the divine permeating every syllable, guiding you towards inner peace, wisdom, and liberation. May these prayers serve as a bridge between the finite and the infinite, leading you on a transformative journey of spiritual growth and awakening. It is my sincere hope that this prayer book becomes a cherished companion on your spiritual path, offering solace in times of need, inspiration in moments of doubt, and a reminder of the profound interconnectedness of all beings. May it ignite the flame of devotion within your heart and inspire you to live a life of virtue, compassion, and service.

With humility and reverence, I offer this collection of prayers to the divine, trusting that its words will resonate with your soul and kindle the sacred fire of devotion within you. May each prayer be a beacon of light on your journey towards self-realization and union with the divine.

May the blessings of the great sages, saints, and deities of Hinduism accompany you on your spiritual quest, guiding you ever closer to the ultimate truth – the realization of your own divine nature.

Namaste

Table of Contents

GAYTREE MANTRA

OM
BHUR BHUVA SVAHA
TAT SAVITUR VARENYAM
BHARGO DEVASYA DHEEMAHI
DHI YO YONAH PRACHODAYAT

O Divine Mother may your pure divine light illuminate
all realms (physical, mental, and spiritual) of our being.
Please expel any darkness from our hearts and bestow
upon us the true knowledge.

Om Shree Ganeshaya Namaha

CHAPTER 1: LORD GANESHA PRAYERS

GANESHA MANTRAS

Vakratunda Ganesha Mantra

OM Vakratund Mahakaya Surya Koti Sama Prabha
    Nirvhignam Kurumedeya Sarva Karyashu Sarvada
*O Ganesha of the curved trunk and massive body,
whose splendour is equal to millions of suns, please
bless us and be kind enough to eradicate all the
obstacles in my endeavours.*

Om Gan Ganapataye namo namaha
Siddhi Vinayaka namo namaha
Astha Vinayaka namo namaha
Ganpati bappa Moriya

Om Gowri Ganesha namo namaha
Parvatee tanaya namo namaha
Lambodharaya namo namaha
Ganapati bappa Moriya

Om Gananathaya namo namaha
Vigneshwaraya namo namaha
Parmeshwaraya namo namaha
Ganapati bappa Moriya

I offer my salutations and bow to you the remover of obstacles.
O God of achievement and enlightenment, I bow to you
O Lord of Wisdom and Happiness, only you make every endeavour and everything possible; You are the remover of all obstacles and you have enchanted every being in the Universe, you are the Lord of all women and all men.

Ganesha Shubh Labh Mantra

Om Shreem Gam Saubhagya Ganpatay
Varvarda Sarvajanma Mein Vashamanya Namah

We ask Lord Ganesha for good fortune and many blessings for our present and future. We offer obeisance to him who blesses long lives, health and happiness.

Ganesha Gayatri Mantra

Om Ekadantaya Viddhamahe, Vakratunda Dhimahi
Tanno Danti Prachodayat.

We pray to Ganesh with the single-tusked elephant tooth as he omnipresent. We meditate upon him and pray for greater intellect. We bow down asking him to illuminate our minds with wisdom

GANESHA CHALISA

Jai Ganapati Sadguna Sadan,
Kavivar Badan Kripaal,
Vighna Haran Mangal Karan,
Jai Jai Girijaalaal [1]
Glory, glory, all glory to you, O Ganesha; to you the
whole world pays homage, for you are the delight of
Gauri and the charming son of Shiva. You are the
extirpator of all pairs of contraries (such as joy and
sorrow, birth and death, attraction and repulsion, etc.)
and deliver from them.

Jai Jai Jai Ganapati Ganaraaju,
Mangal Bharana Karana Shubha Kaajuu,
Jai Gajbadan Sadan Sukhdaata,
Vishva Vinaayaka Buddhi Vidhaataa [2]
Glory to you, O son of Shambhu and delight of Gauri,
you are the destroyer of all obstacles and deliverer of all
from the cycle of birth and death. Glory to you, O leader
of Shiva's henchmen, bestower of happiness on all your
votaries, teacher of all, and operator of the intellect!

VakraTunda Shuchi Shunda Suhaavana,
Tilaka Tripunda bhaal Man Bhaavan,
Raajata Mani Muktana ura maala,
Swarna Mukuta Shira Nayana Vishaalaa [3]
O Ganesha (Vakratunda), resplendent is the only tusk
which you have on your elephant face and well-adorned
is your sacred trunk; the crescent-shaped triple mark
on your forehead is as beautiful as the moon, and the
celestials, men and ascetics who behold your loveliness
cannot off its spell.

Pustak Paani Kuthaar Trishuulam,
Modaka Bhoga Sugandhit Phuulam,
Sundara Piitaambar Tana Saajit,
Charana Paadukaa Muni Man Raajit [4]
On your bosom is a garland of jewels, in your eyes the
beauty of the full-blown lotus and on your head a crown
of gems. You deliver your devotees from anxiety and
wield a sacred axe and a beautiful trident in your
hands. Sweet laddus among delicacies and fragrant
blossoms among flowers are your favourites.

Dhani Shiva Suvan Shadaanana Bhraataa,
Gaurii Lalan Vishva-Vikhyaata,
Riddhi Siddhi Tav Chanvar Sudhaare,
Mooshaka Vaahan Sohat Dvaare [5]
Blessed are you, OKaartikeya's brother and beloved son
of Shiva and Gauri; elegantly attired in a beautiful
yellow silken dress and wearing a pair of wooden
sandals all studded with gems on your feet, you are the
source of all the blessings of the world.

Kahaun Janma Shubh Kathaa Tumhari,
Ati Shuchi Paavan Mangalkaarii,
Ek Samay Giriraaj Kumaarii,
Putra Hetu Tapa Kiinhaa Bhaarii [6]

Both prosperity and accomplishment wave royal
whisks (chowries) over you and your vehicle, the
mouse, adds to your splendour at your door. As the
story of your life is so strange and mysterious, who can
venture to describe your magnificence, which passes all
telling?

Bhayo Yagya Jaba Poorana Anupaa,
Taba Pahunchyo Tuma Dhari Dvija Rupaa,
Atithi Jaani Kay Gaurii Sukhaarii,
Bahu Vidhi Sevaa Karii Tumhaarii [7]
A demon, disguised as Shiva,often came there to delude
Gauri in order to foil his design, Gauri, the beloved
consort of Shiva created a divine form from the scurf of
her body.

Ati Prasanna Hvai Tum Vara Diinhaa,
Maatu Putra Hit Jo Tap Kiinhaa,
Milhii Putra Tuhi, Buddhi Vishaala,
Binaa Garbha Dhaarana Yahi Kaalaa [8]
Asking her son to keep watch, she stationed him at the
palace-door like a doorkeeper. When Shiva himself
came there, he, being unrecognised was denied
entrance into the house.

Gananaayaka Guna Gyaan Nidhaanaa,
Puujita Pratham Roop Bhagavaanaa,
Asa Kehi Antardhyaana Roop Hvai,
Palanaa Par Baalak Svaroop Hvai [9]
Shiva asked: Tell me, who is your father? In a voice
sweet as honey, you replied, Hearken, sir, I am Gauri's
son; don't you dare advance even a step beyond this
point.

BaniShishuRudanJabahiTum Thaanaa,
Lakhi Mukh Sukh Nahin Gauri Samaanaa,

Sakal Magan Sukha Mangal Gaavahin,
Nabha Te Suran Suman Varshaavahin [10]
"O Sir! Let me take my mother's permission before I
allow you to go inside; wrangling with a mere stripling
like me will be of no avail." Not listening to your behest,
Shivaat tempted to rush towards the house, which so
vexed you that you, waxing furious, threw the gauntlet
down.

Shambhu Umaa Bahudaan Lutaavahin,
Sura Munijana Suta Dekhan Aavahin,
Lakhi Ati Aanand Mangal Saajaa,
Dekhan Bhii Aaye Shani Raajaa [11]
In a fit of rage, Shiva picked up his trident and driven
by delusion hurled it on you. Your head, tender like the
Shirisa flower was severed and instantly it soared into
the sky and disappeared there.

Nija Avaguna Gani Shani Man Maahiin,
Baalak Dekhan Chaahat Naahiin,
Girijaa Kachhu Man Bheda Badhaayo,
Utsava Mora Na Shani Tuhi Bhaayo [12]
When Shiva went happily inside where Gauri, daughter
of the Mountain king was sitting, he smilingly asked,
Tell me, Sati how did you give
birth to son?

Kahana Lage Shani Man Sakuchaai,
Kaa Karihau Shishu Mohi Dikhayii,
Nahin Vishvaasa Umaa Ura Bhayauu,
Shani Son Baalak Dekhan Kahyau [13]
On hearing the whole episode, the mystery cleared.
Gauri, though daughter of the great mountain King
(celebrated for immobility) was so moved and
distraught that she fell to the ground and said, " You
have done me a great disfavour, my Lord; Now go and

fetch the severed head of my son from wherever you find it!"

Padatahin Shani Drigakona Prakaashaa,
Baalak Sira Udi Gayo Aakaashaa,
Girajaa Girii Vikala Hvai Dharanii,
So Dukha Dashaa Gayo Nahin Varanii [14]
Shiva, expert in all skills,took his departure accompanied by Vishnu, but having failed to find the head,they brought one of an elephant and placed it upon the trunk and breathed life into it.

Haahaakaara Machyo Kailaashaa,
Shani Kiinhon Lakhi Suta Ko Naashaa,
Turat Garuda Chadhi Vishnu Sidhaaye,
Kaati Chakra So GajaShira Laaye [15]
It was Lord Shiva who named you Shri Ganesha and blessed you with knowledge, wisdom and immortality. You are O Lord, the first among those who are worshiped; you bring joy to the faithful, destroy all obstructions and cause the operation of the intellect.

Baalak Ke Dhada Uupar Dhaarayo,
Praana Mantra Padhi Shankar Daarayo,
Naama'Ganesha'ShambhuTabaKiinhe,
Pratham Poojya Buddhi Nidhi Vara Diinhe [16]
Whosoever remembers you before embarking on any mission finds all his tasks accomplished in the world. The very remembrance of your name brings all happiness without your all-pardoning grace there is no security and well-being anywhere in the world.

Buddhi Pariikshaa Jab Shiva Kiinhaa,
Prithvii Kar Pradakshinaa Liinhaa,
Chale Shadaanana Bharami Bhulaai,
Rache Baithii Tum Buddhi Upaai [17]

*While Sadmukha (your brother Kaartikeya) went flying
on his peacock, you adopted an easier course) without
budging, you scribbled the name of Raama on the
ground and abandoning all   misgivings,
circumnavigated it.*

**Charana Maatu-Pitu Ke Dhara Liinhen,
Tinake Saat Pradakshina Kiinhen
Dhani Ganesha Kahi Shiva Hiye Harashyo,
Nabha Te Suran Suman Bahu Barse [18]**
*(With utmost devotion) you clasped the feet of your
parents and circumnavigated them seven times. Thus,
were you rewarded with the fruit of having
circumnavigated the earth, a feat that made the gods
rain down flowers on you.*

**Tumharii Mahima Buddhi Badaai,
Shesha Sahasa Mukha Sake Na Gaai,
Main Mati Heen Maliina Dukhaarii,
Karahun Kaun Vidhi Vinaya Tumhaarii [19]**
*While dwelling in the hermitage of the sage Durvasa,
Sundardaasa, a devotee of Raama, composed this hymn
to Ganesha in forty verses just as the foremost among
the adepts in the Shiva Purana had done*

**Bhajata 'Raamsundara' Prabhudaasaa,
Jaga Prayaaga Kakraa Durvaasaa,
Ab Prabhu Dayaa Deena Par Keejai,
Apnii Bhakti Shakti Kuchha Deejai [20]**
*The wise who hymn the glory of Ganesha every day are
blessed with supreme bliss. The lord of Shiva's
henchmen who blesses his votaries with wealth,
progeny and happiness also bestows upon them every*

ll Dohaa ll

Shrii Ganesha Yeh Chaalisaa, Paatha Karre Dhara Dhyaan l
Nita Nav Mangala Graha Base, Lahe Jagat Sanmaana ll
Sambandh Apna Sahasra Dash, Rishi panchamii dinesha l
Poorana Chaalisaa Bhayo, Mangala Moorti Ganesha ll

He who repeats this hymn with earnestness is blessed with all felicity
and gracious gifts, the novelty of which grows ever greater, as well as great honour. On the third day of the dark half of the month of Bhaadra in the Vikrama year two thousand and ten (A. D.1953) this hymn in forty verses was completed. Thus has Sundaradaasa demonstrated his unflinching devotion to Lord Ganesha

GANESHA AARTI

Jai Ganesh, Jai Ganesh, Jai Ganesh Deva (2)
Mata Janaki Parvati Pita Mahadeva (2)
Hail to you O, Lord Ganesha, I bow before you. Salutations to the son of Mata Parvati and Lord Mahadeva.

Jai Ganesh, Jai Ganesh, Jai Ganesh Deva (2)
Hail to you O, Lord Ganesha, I bow before you.

Ek Dant Dayavant, Chaar Bhuja Dhaari
Maathe Pe tilaak Sohe, Muse Ki Savari (2)
I bow before you. Salutations to the one who has one tusk, and four hands. The tilaak adorns his forehead, and he is mounted on his Mooshak.

Paan Chadhe, Phool Chadhe, Aur Chadhe Meva

Ladduan Ka Bhog Lage, Sant Kare Seva
Here's offering the betel leaves, the flowers and the
Mewa. Here's offering the laddoos, as the saints serve
him. Hail to you O, Lord Ganesha, I bow before you.

Jai Ganesh, Jai Ganesh, Jai Ganesh Deva
Mata jakki Parvati Pita Mahadeva
Salutations to the son of Mata Parvati and Lord
Mahadeva. He gives vision to the one who is blind, and
good health to the one who is ill

Andhe Ko Aankh Det, Kodhin Ko Kaaya
Baanjhan Ko Putra Det, Nirdhan Ko Maaya
Sur Shaam Sharan Aye, Saphal Ki Je Seva
He showers his blessings on the one who is childless, and
wealth on the poor. As we pray throughout the day and
in the evening, let our prayers bear the fruits

Mata Janaki Parvati Pita Mahadeva
Jai Ganesh, Jai Ganesh, Jai Ganesh Deva
Jai Ganesh, Jai Ganesh, Jai Ganesh Deva
Mata Janaki Parvati Pita
Salutations to the son of Mata Parvati and Lord
Mahadeva. Hail to you O, Lord Ganesha, I bow before
you.

CHAPTER 2: MAA LAKSHMI PRAYERS
LAXMI CHALISA

||DOHA||

Matu Lakshmi kari kripa, karo Hridaya me vas
Manokamna sidh kare purvahu meri aas

||Sourtha||

Yahi more ardas hath jor vinti karon
Sabvidhi karo suyas jaya jnani jagdambika

||Choupayi||

Sindhu suta main sumro tohi, gyan budhi vidya
do mohi ||1-2
Victory to the goddess Lakshmi, who is revered by the
whole universe, Obeisance to the compassionate
mother, who grants all desires.

Tum saman koi nahi upkari, sab vidhi purbahu
aas hamari ||3
Your glory is sung by the gods, saints, and sages, you
are adorned with divine virtues, bestower of
auspiciousness.

Jai Jai Jagat Janani Jagadambaa, Sab Ki Tumahi
Ho Avalambaa II 4
Victory to you, O giver of prosperity, embodiment of
compassion, You dwell in the heart of Vishnu, remover
of sorrow and distress.

Tumahii Ho Ghat Ghat Ki Waasi, Binti Yahi Hamarii Khaasi II 5
Your radiance illuminates the three worlds, exalted and divine, O Lakshmi, you bring joy to all, dispelling darkness with your light.

Jag Janani Jai Sindhu Kumaari, Deenan Ki Tum Ho Hitakaari II 6
You are the beloved consort of Vishnu, the embodiment of purity, Residing in the hearts of devotees, you fulfill their aspirations.

Binvo Nitya Tum Maharani, Kripa Karo Jag Janani Bhavaani II 7
Victory to the goddess of wealth, the divine mother of the universe, you grant liberation and bestow blessings upon those who seek refuge in you.

Kehi Vidhi Stuti Karon Tihaarii, Sudhi Lijain Aparaadh Bisari II 8
You are the ocean of compassion, the refuge of the destitute, O benevolent Lakshmi, you fulfill the desires of your devotees.

Kriapa drishti Chita woh Mam Orii, Jagat Janani Vinatii Sun Mori II 9
Victory to the radiant goddess, the bestower of divine grace, you grant boons and fulfill wishes, removing obstacles and adversity.

Gyaan Buddhi Jai Sukh Ki Daata, Sankat Harahu Hamaare Maata II 10

Obeisance to you, O goddess Lakshmi, the embodiment
of divine beauty, you are worshipped with devotion,
your glory sung by the celestial beings.

**Kshir Sindhu Jab Vishnumathaayo, Chaudah
Ratn Sindhu Mein Paayo II 10**
*Victory to you, O mother Lakshmi, the embodiment of
auspiciousness, you are the source of all prosperity, the
bestower of divine blessings*

**Chaudah Ratn Mein Tum Sukhraasi, Seva Kiyo
Prabhu Banin Daasi II 12**
*2124Your divine form is adorned with divine ornaments
and fragrant garlands, O goddess Lakshmi, you fulfill
the desires of your devotees, granting them liberation*

**Jab Jab Janam Jahaan Prabhu Linhaa, Roop
Badal Tahan Seva Kinhaa II 13**
*Victory to you, O compassionate mother, the dispeller of
darkness and ignorance, O Lakshmi, you are the
beloved consort of Vishnu, the embodiment of divine
grace.*

**Swayam Vishnu Jab Nar Tanu Dhaara, Linheu
Awadhapuri Avataara II 14**
*Your divine presence brings joy and happiness,
dispelling sorrow and despair, O goddess Lakshmi, you
are worshipped with devotion by gods and humans
alike*

**Tab Tum Prakat Janakapur Manhin, Seva Kiyo
Hriday Pulakaahi II 15**
*Victory to the compassionate mother, the embodiment
of divine grace, O Lakshmi, you are the bestower of*

*wealth and prosperity, the dispeller of poverty and
want.*

Apanaya Tohi Antarayaami, Vishva Vidit Tribhuvan Ki Swaami II 16
*Your divine abode is adorned with celestial jewels and
fragrant flowers, O goddess Lakshmi, you grant
abundance and prosperity to those who seek your grace*

Tum Sam Prabal Shakti Nahi Aani, Kahan Tak Mahimaa Kahaun Bakhaani II 17
*Victory to you, O giver of prosperity, the embodiment of
divine beauty, O Lakshmi, you are worshipped with
devotion by gods and humans alike.*

Mann Karam Bachan Karai Sevakaai, Mann Eechhit Phal Paai II 18
*Joy and happiness follow wherever you go, worshiped
by gods and mortals alike, this we know*

Taji Chhal Kapat Aur Chaturaai, Pujahi Vividh Viddhi Mann Laai II 19
*Victory to you, O compassionate mother, the dispeller of
darkness and ignorance, O Lakshmi, you are the
beloved consort of Vishnu, the embodiment of divine
grace.*

Aur Haal Main Kahahun Bujhaai, Jo Yah Paath Karai Mann Laai II 20
*Your abode a celestial sight, beauty beyond compare,
Granting wealth and prosperity, with compassion rare*

Taako Koi Kasht Na Hoi, Mann Eechhit Phal Paavay Soii II 21

Giver of prosperity, beauty beyond compare,
Worshiped with devotion, everywhere.
Traahi- Traahii Jai Duhkh Nivaarini, Trividh Tap
9Bhav Bandhan Haarini II 22
Your divine abode is adorned with celestial jewels and
fragrant flowers, O goddess Lakshmi, you grant
abundance and prosperity to those who seek your
grace.

Jo Yeh Parhen Aur Parhaavay, Dhyan Laga Kar
Sunay Sunavay II 23
Dispeller of darkness, embodiment of grace, Consort of
Vishnu, your radiance we embrace

Taakon Kou Rog Na Sataavay, Putr Aadi Dhan
Sampati Paavay II 24
Joy and happiness follow, dispelling sorrow's plight,
Worshiped with devotion, day and night
Putraheen Dhan Sampati Heena, Andh Badhir
Korhhi Ati Diinaa II 25
Dispeller of poverty, provider of wealth divine,
Abundance you bring, in every shrine.

Vipra Bulaay Kai Paath Karaavay, Shaankaa Dil
Mein Kabhi Na Laavay II 26
Celestial abode adorned with jewels, fragrance
everywhere, Granting abundance and prosperity, with
utmost care.

Path Karaavay Din Chalisa, Taapar Krapaa
Karahin Gaurisaa II 27
Provider of prosperity, beauty divine, Worshiped with
devotion, for eternity's time.

Sukh Sampatti Bahut-Si Paavay, Kami Nanhin Kaahuu Ki Aavay II 28
Your divine abode is adorned with celestial jewels and fragrant flowers, O goddess Lakshmi, you grant abundance and prosperity to those who seek your grace.

Baarah Maash Karen Jo Puja, Tehi Sam Dhanya Aur Nahin Dujaa II 29
Dispeller of darkness, embodiment of grace, Consort of Vishnu, in every sacred place.

Pratidin Paath Karehi Man Manhi, Un sam koi Jag Mein Naahin II 30
Joy and happiness follow, dispelling sorrow's plight, Worshiped with devotion, day and night.
Bahu vidhi Kaya Mein Karahun Baraai, Ley Parikshaa Dhyaan Lagaai II 31
Dispeller of poverty, provider of wealth divine, Abundance you bring, in every shrine

Kari Vishvaas Karay Vrat Naima, Hoi Siddh Upajay Ur Prema II 32
Celestial abode adorned with jewels, fragrance fills the air, Granting abundance and prosperity, with utmost care

Jai Jai Jai Lakshmi Bhavani, Sab Mein Vyaapit Ho Gun khaani II 33
Provider of prosperity, beauty divine, Worshiped with devotion, for eternity's time

Tumhro Tej Prabal Jag Maahin, Tum Sam Kou Dayaalu Kahun Naahin ||34

Divine form adorned with jewels, fragrance fills the air,
Fulfilling desires, with compassion rare

Mohi Anaath Ki Sudhi Ab Lijay, Sannkat Kaati Bhakti Bar Deejay II 35
Dispeller of darkness, embodiment of grace, Consort of Vishnu, in every sacred place.

Bhool chook Karu Shamaa Hamaari, Darshan Deejay Dasha Nihaari II 36
Joy and happiness follow, dispelling sorrow's plight,
Worshiped with devotion, day and night
Bin Darshan Vyaakul Adhikari, Tumhin Akshat Dukh Shatte Bhaari II37
Dispeller of poverty, provider of wealth divine,
Abundance you bring, in every shrine.

Nahin Mohi Gyaan Buddhi Hai Tan Mein, Sab Jaanat Ho Apane Mann Mein II 38
Celestial abode adorned with jewels, fragrance fills the air, Granting abundance and prosperity, with utmost care

Roop Chaturbhuj Karke Dhaaran, Kasht Mor Ab Karahu Nivaaran II 39
Provider of prosperity, beauty divine, Worshiped with devotion, for eternity's time.

Kehi Prakaar Mein Karahun Badai, Gyaan Buddhi Mohin Nahin Adhikaai II 40
Joy and happiness follow, dispelling sorrow's plight,
Worshiped with devotion, day and night

DOHA:
Traahi Traahi Dukh Haarini, Harahu Vegi Sab Traas I
Jayati Jayati Jai Lakshmi, Karahu Shatru Ka Naas II

Ramdas kahayi pukari, karo duur tum vipati humari ||
Matu Lakshmi das par, Karhu daya ki kor

SHREE LAXMI JI KI AARTEE

Om Jai Lakshmi Mata, Maiya Jai Lakshmi Mata
Tumako Nishidin Sevat, Hari Vishnu Vidhata
 Om Jai Lakshmi Mata

Uma Rama Brahmani, Tum Hi Jag-Mata
Surya-Chandrama Dhyavat Naarad Rishi Gata
Om Jai Lakshmi Mata

Durga Roop Niranjani, Sukh Sampatti Data
Jo Koi Tumako Dhyavat, Riddhi-Siddhi Dhan Pata
Om Jai Lakshmi Mata

Tum Patal-Nivasini, Tum Hi Shubhdata |
Karma-Prabhav-Prakashini, Bhavanidhi Ki Trata
Om Jai Lakshmi Mata

Jis Ghar Mein Tum Rahti, Sab Sadgun Aata
Sab Sambhav Ho Jata, Man Nahi Ghabrata
Om Jai Lakshmi Mata

Tum Bin Yagya Na Hote, Vastra Na Koi Pata
Khan-Pan Ka Vaibhav, Sab Tumase Aata

POWERFUL MANTRAS

Om Shri Suryaye Namaha (God of Light)
Om Namo Shivaye Namaha (God of Enlightment)
Om Namo Narayanoye Namaha (God of Happiness and Good Health)
Om Gan Ganpathaye Namaha (God of Success)
Om Durgaye Namaha (God of Protection)
Om Shri Maha Laxmi Namaha (God of Wealth)
Om Him Saraswatiye Namaha (God of Knowledge)
Om Shri Navgraye Namahe (God of Good Luck &

Destiny)

Om Han Hunumantaye Namaha (God of Power)

Om Shri Sai Namaha (God of Prosperity)
Om Pitra Pratnam Namaha (The Blessing of Ancestors)

Swarna Mantra – For Wealth & Health
Om Naranaye – Swarnaye – Hari Om (Repeat 11 times)

Mantra for Prosperity
On Su-Sha – Hum-Bram-Om (Repeat slowly 11 times)

Mantra to remove all obstacles in life
Om Gan-Ganpathaye Namaha (Repeat 11 times)

Powerful Daily Mantras for success (Navgrah/ 9 planets)

Om Shri Suryaye Namaha
Om Shri Chandraye Namaha
Om Shri Mangalaye Namaha
Om Shri Bhuddhaye Namaha

Om Shri Guruvaye Namaha
Om Shri Shukraye Namaha
Om Shri Shanish Charaye Namaha
On Shri Rahave Namaha
Om Shri Ketave Namaha

CHAPTER 3: LORD SHIVA PRAYERS

SHIV STUTI

Shiva hare shiva ram sakhe prabhu
Trividh tap nivaran ho vibho
Aaj janeskwara Yadava pahiman
Shiv hare vijayam kuru mein varam

Kamal lochan ram daya nidhe
Har guru gaj raksahaje gopate
Shivatano bhawa shakar pahiman   Shiv hare ....

Swajan ranjanmangala mandiram
Bhajati te pourusham param padam
Bhagati tasya soukhan parmambhoutam   Shiv hare
....

Jaya Yudhistir valabh bhupate
Jaya jayarjhita pounya payonidhe
Jaya kripa maya krisna namostoute   Shiv hare ....

Bhawa vimochan madav mapate
Sourh vimanasa hansa shiva rate
Janak jarat raghaw rakchamam   Shiv hare ....

Awani mandal mangal maa pate
Jalada soundar ram ramapate
Nigam kirti gounarnaw gayate   Shiv hare ....

Patita pawan naam mayiya lata
Tawa yasho vimalam pari givate
Tadpi madhav maa kimoupekchase   Shiv hare ....

Amarta pardeva ramapate
Vijayetasteva naam ghanopama
Mayi katham kourounarnava jayate Shiv hare ....

AARTI SHIV JI KI

Om jay Shiv Omkara har Shiv Omkara,
Bramha Vishnu Sadashiv ardhangini dhara
Om jay Shiv om kara ....
Glory to you, O Shiva! Glory to you, O Omkaara! May
Brahma, Vishnu and the assembly of other gods,
including the great Lord Shiva, relieve me of my
afflictions.

Ekanan chatouranan panchanan raje,
Hansanan garourasan vrishvahan saje ......
Om Shiv om kara ...
Being the Absolute, True being, Consciousness and
Bliss, you play the roles of all the three Gods - Brahma,
Vishnu, and Shiva. As Vishnu, you have but one face, as
Brahma four and as Shiva five. They gladden the sight
of all who behold them. As Brahma you prefer the back
of the swan for your seat, as Vishnu you like to ensconce
yourself on the back of Garuda and as Shiva you make
the sacred bull your conveyance, all these stands ready.
O Great Lord, pray rid me of my afflictions!

Do bhouj chatourbhouj dass bhoujate sohe,
Tinon roop nirakhta tribhouwan jan mohe ......
Om Shiv om kara....
As Brahma, you possess two arms, as Vishnu four and
as Shiva (Dashabaahu) ten, all of which look
matchlessly lovely. No sooner do the inhabitants of the
three spheres behold you than they are all enchanted. O
great Lord Omkaara, pray rid me of my afflictions.

Akshmala vanmala moundmala Dhari,
Chandan mrigmad sohebhole Shashi Dhari......
Om Shiv om kara....

You are, O great Lord Omkaara, wearing a garland of Rudraaksha, another of forest flowers the third of skulls; your forehead, glistening in the moonlight which it holds, is smeared with sandal-paste and musk. Pray rid me of my afflictions.

Swetambar pitambar bandhambar ange,
Sankadik bramhadik bhoutadil sange......
Om Shiv om kara....
O great Lord Omkaara, your body is attired in white and yellow silken clothes and in tiger skin, while in your company are troops of goblins, gods like Brahma and divine seers like Sanaka. Pray rid me of my afflictions.

Kar mein shest kamandal chakr trishoul dharta,
Jagkarta jagharta, jagpalan karta ....
Om Shiv om kara....
O great Lord Omkaara, you hold akamandalu (the mendicants water-jar) in one of your hands and in another a trident; you bring joy to all, destroy all distress and sustain the whole world. May you rid me of all my afflictions!

Bharma Vishnu Sadashiv janat aviveka,
Pranakshar ke madye yaha tinon eka ......
Om Shiv om kara....
The ignorant (unwise and stupid) know Brahma, Vishnu and Shiva as three individual gods, but they are all indistinguishably fused into a single mystic syllable 'OM'. Pray rid me of my afflictions.

Trigoun Shiv ki aarti koyi gawe,
Kahat shivanand swami manvanchit phal pawe
......
Om Shiv om kara....

Says Swami Shivananda, "He who recites this Arti to the Lord of the three gunas-sattva, rajas and tamas - attains fulfilment of his heart's desire". O great Lord Omkaara, may you rid me of my afflictions.

MRITYUR JAI MANTRA

Om trayam bakam yajamahey
Sugandhi poosti vardhanaam
Ourya ruk mew vandanaam
Mritior mukshit mamritat.

The three-eyed one we adore, honour and worship.
Sweet fragrance, A fullness of life.
One who nourishes and strengthens health and wealth.
Liberate from death - immortality.

Tryambakam Mantra, *is a prayer offered to the ancient deities viz. Indra, Varuna, and Mitra. This prayer is recitation of names to Lord Shiva and is believed to overcome death to nourish and nurture human beings from all illness and diseases.*

SHIV-GANGA BHAJAN

Shivji par charhela ganga ke jalwaa
Ganga ke jalwaa ho, ganga kejalwaa, ho ......
Dam dam bajela Shivji ke damruwa,

Shivji ke damruwa ho, Shivji kr damruwa, ho
Nachela jhumela O bhole baba, (3)
Ho.... ho.....ho....ho....

CHAPTER 4: MAA DURGA PRAYERS

SHAKTI VANDANA

Jay Ambe Doorga maiya, jay magala murati maiya, jay Ananda karni
Jay Ambe Luxmee maiya, jay magal murati maiya, jay Ananda karni
Jay Ambe Gayatree maiya, jay magala murati maiya, jay Ananda karni
Jay Ambe Saraswatee maiya, jay magala murati maiya, jay Ananda karni
Jay Ambe Gawree maiya, jay magala murati maiya. Jay Ananda karni
Jay Ambe Mohini maiya, jay magala murti maiya, jay Ananda karni.

DOORGA RAMAN

Jish desh main jish bhesh main jish dham mein raho
Doorga raman doorga raman doorga raman kaho

Jish raag mein enuraag mein ya virag mein raho
Doorga raman doorga raman doorga raman kaho

Rishikesh mein hari dwar mein ya shuktaar mein raho
Doorga raman doorga raman doorga raman kaho
Jish marg mein jish roop mein jish kaam mein raho
Doorga raman doorga raman doorga raman kaho

JAGDAMBA BHAJAN

Dware tiharee bari bhir jagdamba maya
Dware tihare bari bhir jagdamba maiya

Dware tiharee balak phukare,
Balak phukare bari bheer
Jagdamba maya, Dware tiharee ....

Dware tihare kanya phukare
Kanya phukare bari bheer
Jagdamba maya Dware tiharee ....

Dware tihare santana phukare,
Santanan phukare bari bheer
Jagdamba maya Dware tiharee ....

Andhe ko nainan banjeen ko balak,
Andhe ko naina bari bheer
Jagdamba maya, Dware tiharee ....

SHAKTEE MANTRAS

Ya devi sarva bhoutesoo Shaktee roopey nasansita
Namastasye Namastasye Namastasye namo namaha

Now you just have to replace the word **Shaktee** with:
"Vishnu Mayatee", "Chatanya Bhudhiyate", "Budhi",
"Nindra", "Skudha", "Chaya", "Trishna", "Kshanti",
"Jati", "Laaja", "Santi", "Shradha", "Kanti", "Lashimi",
"Vritee", "Shmritee", "Daya", "Tushti", "Matri", "Branti",
"Doorga", "Kali", "Pritvi", "Mukti", "Jyoti" & "Ganga"

SHREE DOORGA CHALISA

DOHA:
*Sarva Mangal mangalye, Shivey sarvad
sadhike
Sharanyey trayambakey gowri, Narayani
namoustoutey*

**Namo Namo Durge Sukh karani, Namo Namo
ambe Dukh harani.[1]**

*Salutations and Salutations to Durga, the giver of
pleasure,
Salutations and salutations to the remover of Sorrow.*

**Nirakar hai jyoti tumhari, Tihun lok pheli
ujayari [2]
Shashi lalat mukh mahavishala, Netra lal
bhrikutee vikarala.[3]**

*Your radiance is unparalleled, and you shed light on the
three worlds. Your face is like a moon and mouth very
broad, your eyes are red and your frown frightening.*

**Roop Matu ko adhika sohawe, Darasha karata
jana ahtisukha pawe. [4]**
**Tum sansar shakti laya kina, Palan hetu anna
dhan dina. [5]**
*Oh mother, you are extremely pretty, and a sight of you
brings pleasure to all. In you is merged the strength of
this world, And you provide it with food and wealth.*

**Annapurna hui jag pala, Tumhi Adi sundari
Bala. [6]**
**Pralaya kala sab nashan hari, Tum gauri Shiv-
Shankar pyari. [7]**
*As Annapurni you nurture the world, and you are the
primeval beauty called Bala. During deluge you destroy
everything, And you are Gauri the darling of Shiva
Shankara*

**Shiv yogi tumhre guna gaven, Brahma Vishnu
tumhen nit dhyaven. [8]**
**Roop Saraswati ko tum dhara, De subuddhi rishi
munina ubara. [9]**
*The saints of Shiva sing your praises, And Brahma and
Vishnu daily meditate on you. You also take the form of
Saraswathi And grant them wisdom and look after
them.*

**Dharyo roop Narsimha ko amba, Pragat bhayin
phar kar khamba. [10]**
**Raksha kari Prahlaad bachayo, Hiranakush ko
swarga pathayo. [11]**

*Oh mother you take the form of Man - lion, And broke
the pillar and became visible. You saved the Prahlada
and, Sent Hiranyakashipu to heaven.*

**Lakshmi roop dharo jag mahin, Shree Narayan
anga samihahin. [12]**
**Ksheer sindhu men karat vilasa, Daya Sindhu
deeje man asa. [13]**
*You take the form of Goddess Lakshmi And found
reposing with Lord Narayan. You came out of the ocean
of milk, Oh sea of mercy, please fulfil my wishes.*

**Hingalaja men tumhin Bhavani, Mahima amit na
jat bakhani. [14]**
**Matangi Dhoomavati Mata, Bhuvneshwari
baggalas sukhdata. [15]**
*Oh Bhavani, you are the one in Hingalaja, and your
great power is beyond description. You yourself are
Mathangi and mother Dhoomavathi,
You yourself are Bhuveneswari and Bhagalamukhi.*

**Shree Bhairav Tara jag tarani, Chhinna Bhala
bhav dukh nivarani. [16]**
**Kehari Vahan soh Bhavani, Langur Veer Chalat
agavani. [17]**

*As Bhairavi and Tara you redeem the world, and you
are also Chinnamastha, the panacea of sorrows. You
repose gracefully on your steed and are welcomed by
the hero of Monkeys.*

**Kar men khappar khadag viraje, Jako dekh kal
dan bhaje. [17]**
**Sohe astra aur trishoola, Jate uthata shatru hiya
shoola. [18]]**

*When with a sword and a head you appear, it is seen
that even time runs in panic. Seeing with weapons and
the trident, The heart of the enemy trembles with fear.*

**Nagarkoti men tumhi virajat, Tihun lok men
danka bajat. [19**
**Shumbhu Nishumbhu Danuja tum mare, Rakta-
beeja shankhan samhare. [20]**

*You only shine in Nagarkot, And all the three worlds
shudder. You killed the brothers Shumbha and
Nishumba, and also killed the crowds of Raktha Bheeja.*

**Mahishasur nripa ati abhimani, Jehi agha bhar
mahi akulani. [21]**
**Roop karal Kalika dhara, Sen Sahita tum hin
samhara. [22]**
*Mahishasura was king who was proud, who filled the
earth with his sins, And you took the ferocious form of
Kali, And killed him along with his army.*

**Pari garha Santan par jab jab, Bhayi sahaya Maa
tum tab tab. [24]**
**Amarpuni aru basava loka, Tava Mahima sab
rahen asoka. [25]**
*Whenever the saints are in trouble, You mother came to
their rescue. All the words including that of devas,
Remain sorrow less, only by your grace.*

**Jwala men hai jyoti tumhari, Tumhen sada
poojen nar nari. [26]**
**Prem bhakti se Jo yash gave, Dukh-daridra nikat
nahin ave [27]**
*In the goddess jwalamukhi is your light, and all men
and women always pray you. They who sing about you*

with loving devotion, Will never be neared by sorrow or poverty.

Dhyave tumhen jo nar man laee, Janam-maran tako chuti jaee. [28]
Jogi sur-muni kahat pukari, Jog na ho bin shakti tumhari [29]
He who meditates you in his mind, Will get rid of the cycle of birth and death. Yogis, devas and sages openly say, they cannot get salvation without you

Shankar Aacharaj tap keenhon, Kam, krodha jeet sab leenhon. [30]
Nisidin dhyan dharo Shankar ko, Kahu kal nahini sumiro tum ko. [31]
Adhi Shankara did penance on you And won over desire and anger. He always meditated on Lord Shiva, and never spent any time on you.

Shakti roop ko maran na payo, Shakti gayi tab man pachitayo. [32]
Sharnagat hui keerti bakhani, Jai jai jai Jagdamb Bhavani. [33]
Since he did not realize your powers, He became sorry because his powers waned. Then he sought your protection and sung your praise, Victory, victory, victory to Bhavani mother of the world.

Bhayi prasanna Aadi Jagdamba, Dayi shakti nahin keen vilamba. [34]
Mokon Matu kashta ati ghero, Tum bin kaun hare dukh mero. [35]
Then the primordial mother of the world was pleased, And gave him back his powers immediately. Severe distress afflicts me, and who else can kill my sorrow,

except you.

Aasha trishna nipat sataven, Moh madadik sab binsaven. [36]
Shatru nash keeje Maharani, Sumiron ekachita tumhen Bhavani. [37]
Desire and longing always torture me, And passions and lust torment my heart. Oh great queen kill all my enemies, For I meditate with one mind on you.

Karo kripa Hey Matu dayala, Riddhi-Siddhi de karahu nihala. [38]
Jab lagi jiyoon daya phal paoon, Tumhro yash mein sada sunaoon. [39]
Please show me mercy, my kind mother, And show me the paths to riches and powers. As long as I live may I get your mercy, And I would make others hear your fame.

Durga Chalisa jo gave, Sab sukh bhog parampad pave [40]
Devidass sharan nij jani, karahu kripa jagdamb Bhavani
He who sings these forty verses on Durga,
Will receive all happiness and attain salvation.

PRAYER TO MAHA KALI

Jayanti mangala Kali, Bhadra Kali kapalinee
Doorga sma Shiva dhatree, Swaha swadha
namoustoutey.

DEVI PUJA

Om Namaschandikaaye
Jayanti Mangala Kaalee
Bhadrakaalee kapaalinee
Durgaa kshaamaa shiwaa dhaatree
Swaahaa Swadhaa namostute

Roopam dehi jayam dehi
yasho dehi dwisho jahi
Sarva swarupe sarveshe
sarva shakti samanvite
Bhawe bhyaastraahino devi
Durge devi namo stu te
Naaraayani Namostute
Siddhi buddhi pradhe devi
bhukti mukti pradaayani
Mantra moorthe mahaadevi
Mahaalakshmee namo stute
Sarwaa baadhaa bineer
mukto dhana dhaanya sutaa nito
Manushyo mat prasaadeno
bhavishyaiti na sanshayaha

KIRTAN DOORGA JI KI

Doorga jin ka naam hein, sarvatra jin ka dham hein.
Eise maa jagdamba ko baram bar pranam hein.
Doorga jin ka naam hein.....

Sinha jin ka vahan hein, jaag mein jin ka shasan hein
Eise Doorga maa ko baram bar pranam hein
Doorga jin ka naam hein

Satyavrat ko gyan sikhaya, purushukta ko niti parayo
Eise Saraswatee maa ko baram bar pranam hein
Doorga jin ka naam hein ....

Dev danawa ke yudh mitayo, Indra ko updesh sunayo
Eise chandee maa ko baram bar pranam hein
Doorga jin ka naam hein ....

Mahishasur ko mar geerayo, Raktabij ka sanhar kiyo
Eise Gawree maa ko baram bar pranam hein
Doorga jin ka hein ....

Treetap se maa hame bachayo, hum sab ka oudhar karo
Eise shakti maa ko baram bar pranam hein
Doorga jin ka naam hein ....

AARTEE

Karpur gawram karoona vataram, Sansara saram
boojagendraharam
Sada vasantam hirday ravinde, Bhawam bhawanee
sahitam namamee

Aartee

Mangal ki sewa souno Doorga Mayya (2)
Aya tere dwar baram bar namaskar mayya ....

Jaya Janani jaya mata Bhawani,
Aya tere dwar baram bar namaskar mayya....

Doorga doorg vinashini mayya
Touhi Laxmi mata,aya tere dwar baram bar ......

Mangal ki sewa souno Doorga mayya ......

MAA DOORGA AARTEE

Aartee Doorga Bhawani ki, ke jay jay Shiv maharani ki
Gale mein pushpin ki mala, Hanth mein trishul aur bala
Jay apne chakra sudarshan se, outare bhaar Bhoomi
tarka
Kamal se nayan, kehri yajan, paro re sharan
Ye devi mukti anand ki, ke jay jay Shiv maharani ki,
Aartee Doorga Bhawani ki......

Yehai Shankar ki maha Gowri, Yeh hai Bram bha ki
maya
Yehi hai Vishnu ki Shakti, bari piyari, bari niyari, Jhalak
bhari
Ye devi Dev Gaja nand ki, ke jay jay Shiv Maharani ki,
Aartee Doorga Bhawani ki......

Liya hai navroop ka avtar, kiya hai sabka bera paar
Ye maiya sare jag ka saar, Sherawali, Kapar wali Maha
kali
Yehi Devi jag santan ki, ke jay jay Shiv maharani ki,
Aartee Doorga bhawani ki.......

DOORGA MATA KI AARTEE

Ambe tou hein Jagdambe kali,
Jay Doorga Khapparwali
Tere hi goon gayein bhaarati
O Mayyaa ham sab Ootarein teri aarti

Tere bhakta jannon par mata, bhir pari hein bhaari
Danav dal par toot paro maa, Karke shinha savari
Saw saw shinhon se balshaali, hein tou dash bhoojaa
wali,
Dookhyon ke doukhare, nivarati,

O Mayya, ham sab ootarein teri aarti

Maa bete ka hein iss jag mein, bara hi nirmal naata,
Poot kapoot soone hein par naa, Matta souni koomata,
Sab pay karuna darshaane wali, amrit varshaane wali,
Dookhyou ke dookhre nivaarti
O Mayya, ham sab ootaare teri aarti

Nahi maangte dhan aur Dawlat, naa chandi naa sona
Ham to maangte Maa, tere man mein, ek chota sa konaa,
Sab ki bigri banana wali, laaj bachaane wali
Satiyon ke sat ko sawaarti,
O Mayya, ham sab ......(bis)

AARTEE JAI AMBE MATA KI

➤ Om jai ambe Gauri maiya, Jai Shyam gauri
   Nishdina tumko dhyavat, Hari Brahma Shivji,
Om   Jai Ambe ...

➤ Mang sindoor birajat tiko mrigh madko, Ujjval se
   do naina
   Chandra vadan niko, om jai Ambe gauri ...

➤ Kanak sanam kalevar, Raktambar raje, Rakta
   pushpa galmala
   Kanth par saje, Om jai ambe ......

➤ Kehari vahan rajat, khadag khappar dhari
   Soor nar munijan sevat, thinke dookhahari, Om
jai Ambe ......

➤ Kanan kundal shobhit, nasagre moti, kotik
   Chandra Divakar

Samnajat Joyti, Om jai Ambe ......

- ➤ Shoombha-nishoomba vidare, Mahishasoor ghati
  Dhoomra Vilochan naina, nishdin madmati, Om
  jai Ambe ......

- ➤ Brahmani Rudrani toom kamala rani, Aagam-
  nigam bakhani
  Tum Shiv patarani, Om jai Ambe ....

- ➤ Chawsath yogini gavat, nritya, karat bhairon,
  bajat tal mridanga
  Aur bajat damru, Om jai Ambe ....

- ➤ Tum ho jag ki mata, tum hi ho Bharata, bhaktan
  ki dookh harta
  Sookh sampati karta, Om jai Ambe ......

- ➤ Bhuja char ati shobhit, var mudra dhari,
  Manvanchit phal pavat
  Sevat naar nari, Om jai Ambe ....

- ➤ Kanchan thal virajat, agaru kapur bati, Malketu
  mein rajat
  Kotinatan jyoti, Om jai Ambe ......

- ➤ Shri Ambe ji ki aarti, jo koyi nara gawe, Kahata
  Shivanand Swami
  Sook sampati pawe, Om jai Ambe ......

CHAPTER 5: LORD KRISHNA PRAYERS

NARAYAN BHAJAN

Bhajaman Narayan Narayan Narayan
He naath Narayan Vasudeva
Shriman Narayan Narayan Narayan
Luxmee Narayan Narayan Narayan
Sourya Narayan Narayan Narayan
Badri Narayan Narayan Narayan
Gunpath Narayan Narayan Narayan

SHYAM TERI BANSI

Shyam teri bansi baje dhire dhire
Baje dhire dhire shri Yamuna ji ke tire
Ita Mathura uta Gokula nagari
Bicha me Yamuna bahe dhire dhire

Ita madhumangala uta shridaama
Bicha me Radha chale dhire dhire

Ita me Lalita uta me vishakha
Bicha me kaanha chale dhire dhire

Ham saba aaye teri sharana me
Hamko bhi darshan milen dhire dhire.

SHREE KRISHNA BHAJAN

Shyam dil bekarar tere bina
Koyi poochena hai tere bina

Shyam dekho hamari ankhei

Houwi ro-ro ke lal tere bina (Shyam ...)

Shyam dekho tumhari Radha
Rahe hardam udass tere bina, (Shyam ....)
Shyam deho tumhari gaouein
Yeh to khaye nag has tere bina (Shyam ....)

Shyam dekho toumahi gopiyan
Yep, to nache na ras tere bina, (Shyam ....)

Shyam dekho toumare gwale
Khaye maakhan na aaj tere bina. (Shyam ....)

Shyam dekho yah matta Yashoda
Yeh to rirke na chach etre bina (Shyam ....)

Shyam dekho yah Vrinda-Mathur
Sunna Yamuna ka ghat tere bina. (Shyam ....)

SHREE KRISHNA AARTI

Aarti Koonja Beehari Ki Shree Giridhar Krishna Murari
Ki
Gale me vaijanti maalaa, bajawe murli Madhura baalaa
Shrawana mei koondala jalkalaa, nanda ke aananda
nandalaalaa
Gangana sama anga kanti kaali, raadhika chamaka rahi
aali
Latana main thaadaya banmali
Bhramar so alak, kastouri teeluck, chanda si jhalaka.....
Lalita chabi shyamaa pyarri ki, Shree Giridhara ......

Kanaka manya mora makuta bilsen, devata darshana ko
tarsen,

Gangana son soomana raasi barsen
Baje murchanga, Madhura mridanga, gwalina ke sanga
Atool raati gopa kumara ki, Shree Giridhara ....

Jahan se pragata bhayi gangaa, kulas haarini shree
gangaa,
Smaran te hota moha bhangaa
Basi Shiv seesha, jataa ke bich, hare adha kicha
Charan chabi Shri banwaari ki, shree Giridhar ....

VISHNU JI KI AARTEE

Aum jai Jagadish hare, swami jai Jagadish hare
Bhakta janon ke sankat kshan mein dour kare
Aum jai Jagadish hare .....

Jo dyawa phal pawe dookh vinesh man ka
Sookh sampati ghar awe kasht mite tan ka,
Aum jai Jagadish hare .....

Mata pita toum mere sharan gahon mein kiski
Toum bin aur na dooja ass karoun mein jiski
Aum jai Jagadish hare .....

Toum pouranparmatma toum antaryami
Parbramha Parmeshwar toum sab ke swami
Aum jai Jagadish hare .....

Toum karuna ke sagar toum plan karta
Mein sewak toum swami kripa karo bharta
Aum jai Jagadish hare .....

Tou mho ek agochar sab ke pran pati
Kisse vidhi miloun dayamaye toum ko mein koumati

Din bandoo dookh harta toum rakshak mere
Karuna hasta bharawa sharan para tere
Aum jai Jagadish hare .....

Vishay vicar mitawo pap haro dewa
Sharadha bhaktibaraho santana ki sewa
Aum jai Jagadish hare .....

Tan man dhan sab hai tera, swami sab kuch hai tera
Tera tujhko Arpan, kya laage mera
Aum jai Jagadish hare .....

Aum jai Jagadish hare, swami jai Jagadish hare
Bhakta janon ke sankat kshan mein dour kare....
Aum jai Jagadish hare .....

BHAGAWAT BHAJAN

Shree Krishna Govind hare murari, he naath Narayan
Vasudeva
Keshav jay jay Madhawa jay jay, he naath narayn
Vasudeva
Govinda jaya jya Gopal jay jay, radha Ramn Hari Govind
jay jay
Aum namo Bhagwatey Vasudevaya, Shiv Shiv Shiv on
namh Shivay

MAHA MANTRA

Maha mantra yaha hai, japa kar japa kar
Hare Ram Ram, Hare Krishna Krishna

Doustho ne lohe ka kambha racha tha
To nirdosh Prahalad kaisse bachaa tha
Pukara yahi naam hirdaye se ousne
Hare Krishna Krishna, Hare Krishna Krishna

Laggi aag lanka mein, halchal machi thi
Vibhishan ki kouthiya to kaisse bachi thi
Likha tha yahi naam kouthiya ke oupar
Hare Ram Ram, Hare Ram Ram

Kaho nath Sewri ke ghar kaisse aye
Aur aye to joothi ber khaye kioun
Jaban par yahi tha hirday par yehi tha
Hare Ram Ram, Hare ram Ram

Puchi thi vo ek din Himachal koumari
Kaho nath kaun mantra kalyan kari
To bole Mahadeo Sambhu Trilochan
Hare Ram Ram, Hare Krishna Krishna

Sabha mein khari Dropadi ro rahi thi
Roro ke ansu se mukh dho rahi thi
Pukara yahi naam hirday se ousene
Hare Krishna Krishna, Hare Krishna Krishna
Maha Mantra ....

CHAPTER 6: LORD RAM PRAYERS

RAM BHAJAN (1)

Sita Ram kaho Radhe Shyam kaho
Radhe Shyam kaho Sita Ram Kaho
Sita Ram bina sukha kaun kare
Radhe Shyam bina dookha kaun hare

RAM BHAJAN (2)

Kabhi Ram Banke Kabhi Shyam Banke
Chale Aana Prabhu Ji Chale Aana
Kabhi Ram Banke Kabhi Shyam Banke
Chale Aana Prabhu Ji Chale Aana

Tum Ram Roop Mein Aana (2)
Sita Saath Leke, Dhanush Haat Leke
Chale Aana Prabhu Ji Chale Aana
Kabhi Ram Banke Kabhi Shyam Banke
Chale Aana Prabhu Ji Chale Aana

Tum Shyam Roop Mein Aana (2)
Radha Saath Leke, Murli Haat Leke
Chale Aana Prabhu Ji Chale Aana
Kabhi Ram Banke Kabhi Shyam Banke
Chale Aana Prabhu Ji Chale Aana

Tum Shiv Ke Roop Mein Aana (2)
Gouri Saath Leke, Damru Haat Leke
Chale Aana Prabhu Ji Chale Aana
Kabhi Ram Banke Kabhi Shyam Banke
Chale Aana Prabhu Ji Chale Aana

Tum Vishnu Roop Mein Aana (2)
Lakhsmi Saath Leke, Chakra Haat Leke
Chale Aana Prabhu Ji Chale Aana
Kabhi Ram Banke Kabhi Shyam Banke
Chale Aana Prabhu Ji Chale Aana

Tum Ganapati Roop Mein Aana (2)
Riddhi Saath Leke, Siddhi Saath Leke
Chale Aana Prabhu Ji Chale Aana
Kabhi Ram Banke Kabhi Shyam Banke
Chale Aana Prabhu Ji Chale Aana

Kabhi Ram Banke Kabhi Shyam Banke
Chale Aana Prabhu Ji Chale Aana
Kabhi Ram Banke Kabhi Shyam Banke
Chale Aana Prabhu Ji Chale Aana

...

RAGOOPATI RAGAVA......

Ragoopati Ragav Raja Ram
Patit Pawan Sita Sita Ram (2)
Sita Ram Sita Ram
Bhaj pyare tou Sita Ram
Ragoopati ....

Ishwar prabhu ji tero neem
Sab ko samati de Bhagwan
Raggopati ....

Bhajley Bhajaley Sita Ram
Mangal moorti Radhey Shyam
Ragoopati ....

Gaht mein tulsi mouk mein Ram
Jay bolo jay Sita Ram
Ragoopati ....

Haathon se karo ghar ka kaam
Mookh se bolo Sita Ram
Ragoopati ....

Saryu kinare ayodya dham
Waha basaat hein Sita Ram
Ragoopati ....

Jay Ragoonandan Jay Siya Ram
Jaanki Valaab Sita Ram
Ragoopati ....

‖ Doha ‖

Shri guru charan saroj raj neej manu mukur sudhari
Baranu raghubar bimal jasu jo dayaku phal chari

Taking the dust of my Guru's lotus feet to polish the mirror of my heart,
I sing the pure fame of the best of Raghus, which bestows the four fruits of life.

Buddhi heen tanu janike sumero pavan kumar
Bal buddhi bidya deu mohi harau kales bikar

I don't know anything, so I remember you, Son of the Wind.
Grant me strength, intelligence and wisdom and remove my impurities and sorrows.

‖ Chaupayee ‖

Jai Hanuman gyan gun sagar ‖
Jai kapis tihu lok ujagar ‖ o 1 ‖
Hail Hanuman, ocean of wisdom/Hail Monkey Lord! You light up the three worlds

Ram doot atulit bal dhama ‖
Anjaani-putra pavan sut nama ‖ o 2 ‖
You are Ram's messenger, the abode of matchless power/ Anjani's son, "Son of the Wind."

Mahabir bikram Bajrangi ‖
Kumati nivar sumati ke sangi ‖ o 3 ‖
Great hero, you are a mighty thunderbolt/Remover of evil thoughts and companion of the good

Kanchan baran biraj subesa ‖
Kanan kundal kunchit kesa ‖ o 4 ‖
Golden hued and splendidly adorned/with heavy earrings and curly locks.

Hath bajra aur dhvaja biraje ‖
Kaandhe munj janeu saje ‖ o 5 ‖
In your hands shine mace and a banner/a sacred thread adorns your shoulder.

Sankar suvan Kesari nandan ‖

Tej pratap maha jag bandan ‖ 06 ‖
You are an incarnation of Shiva and Kesari's son/Your glory is revered throughout the world.

Bidyavaan guni ati chatur ।
Ram kaj karibe ko aatur ‖ 07 ‖
You are the wisest of the wise, virtuous and very clever/ ever eager to do Ram's work.

Prabhu charitra sunibe-ko rasiya ।
Ram Lakhan Sita maan basiya ‖ 08 ‖
You delight in hearing of the Lord's deeds/ Ram, Lakshman and Sita dwell in your heart.

Sukshma roop dhari Siyahi dikhava ।
Bikat roop dhari Lank jarava ‖ 09 ‖
Assuming a tiny form you appeared to Sita/ in an awesome form you burned Lanka.

Bhim roop dhari asur sahare ।
Ramachandra ke kaj savare ‖ 10 ‖
Taking a dreadful form you slaughtered the demons/completing Lord Ram's work.

Laye sanjivan Lakhan jiyaye ।
Shri Raghuvir harashi ur laye ‖ 11 ‖
Bringing the magic herb you revived Lakshman/ Shri Ram embraced you with delight.

Raghupati kinhi bahut badhaee ।
Tum mam priye Bharat-hi-sam bhai ‖ 12 ‖
The Lord of the Raghus praised you greatly/"You are as dear to me as my brother Bharat!"

Sahas badan tumharo jas gaave |
Asa-kahi Shripati kantha lagave || 13 ||
Thousands of mouths will sing your fame!"/ So saying
Lakshmi's Lord drew you to Himself.

Sankadik brahmadi munisa |
Narad-sarad sahit ahisa || 14 ||
Sanak and the sages, Brahma, and the munis/ Narada,
Saraswati and the King of serpents,

Jum Kuber digpaal jaha teh |
Kabi Kovid kahi sake kahan teh || 15 ||
Yama, Kubera, the guardians of the four quarters/poets
and scholars-none can express your glory.

Tum upkar Sugreevahi keenha |
Ram milaye rajpad deenha || 16 ||
You did great service for Sugriva/ bringing him to
Ram, you gave him kingship.

Tumharo mantra Vibhishan maana |
Lankeshvar bhaye sab jag jana || 17 ||
Vibhishana heeded your counsel/He became the Lord of
Lanka, as the whole world knows

Yug sahastra jojan par bhanu |
Leelyo tahi madhur phaal janu || 18 ||
Though the sun is millions of miles away/ you
swallowed it thinking it to be a sweet fruit.

Prabhu mudrika meli mukh mahi |
Jaladi langhi gaye achraj nahi || 19 ||

Holding the Lord's ring in your mouth/ it's no surprise that you leapt over the ocean.

Durgaam kaj jagat ke jete |
Sugam anugraha tumhre tete || 2 0 ||
Every difficult task in this world becomes easy by your grace.

Ram duwaare tum rakhvare |
Hoat na adyna binu paisare || 2 1
You are the guardian at Ram's door/ no one enters without your permission.

Sab sukh lahe tumhari sarna |
Tum rakshak kahu ko darna || 2 2 ||
Those who take refuge in you find all happiness/ those who you protect know no fear.

Aapan tej samharo aape |
Teenho lok hank teh kanpe || 2 3 ||
You alone can withstand your own splendor/ the three worlds tremble at your roar.

Bhoot pisaach nikat nahin aave |
Mahabir jab naam sunave || 2 4 ||
Ghosts and goblins cannot come near/ Great Hero, when your name is uttered.

Nase rog hare sab peera |
Japat nirantar Hanumant beera || 2 5 ||
All disease and pain is eradicated/ by constantly repeating of your name, brave Hanuman.

Sankat se Hanuman chudave |
Man karam bachan dyan jo lave || 26 ||
Hanuman, you release from affliction all those/ who
remember you in thought word and deed.

Sab par Ram tapasvee raja |
Teen ke kaj sakal tum saja || 27 ||
Ram, the ascetic king, reigns over all/ but you carry out
all his work.

Aur manorath jo koi lave |
Sohi amit jeevan phal pave || 28 ||
One who comes to you with any yearning/ obtains the
abundance of the Four Fruits of Life.

Charo yug partap tumhara |
Hai parasiddha jagat ujiyara || 29 ||
Your splendor fills the four ages/ your glory is
renowned throughout the world.

Sadhu sant ke tum rakhware |
Asur nikanandan Ram dulare || 30 ||
You are the guardian of saints and sages/ the destroyer
of demons and the darling of Ram.

Ashta-sidhi nav nidhi ke daata |
Asabar deen Janki mata || 31 ||
You grant the eight powers and nine treasures/ by the
boon you received from Mother Janaki.

Ram rasayan tumhare pasa |
Sada raho Raghupati ke dasa || 32 ||

*You hold the elixir of Ram's name/ and remain
eternally his servant.*

**Tumhare bhajan Ram ko paave |
Janam-janam ke dukh bisrave ‖ 33 ‖**
*Singing your praise, one finds Ram/ and the sorrows of
countless lives are destroyed.*

**Anth-kaal Raghubar pur jaee |
Jaha janma Hari-bhakht kahaee ‖ 34 ‖**
*At death one goes to Ram's own abode/ born there as
God's devotee.*

**Aur devta chitta na dharaee |
Hanumanth se he sarba sukh karaee ‖ 35 ‖**
*Why worship any other deities/ from Hanuman you'll
get all happiness.*

**Sankat kate-mite sab peera |
Jo sumire Hanumat balbeera ‖ 36 ‖**
*All affliction ceases and all pain is removed/ for those
who remember the mighty hero, Hanuman.*

**Jai Jai Jai Hanuman gosaee |
Krupa karahu gurudev ki naee ‖ 37 ‖**
*Victory, Victory, Victory Lord Hanuman/ bestow your
grace on me, as my Guru!*

**Jo sath baar paath kar koi |
Chuthee bandhi maha sukh hoee ‖ 38 ‖**
*Whoever recites this a hundred times/ is released from
bondage and gains bliss.*

Jo yaha padhe Hanuman Chalisa |
Hoye Siddhi Sakhi Gaurisa || 39 ||
One who reads this Hanuman Chalisa/ gains success,
as Gauri's Lord (Shiva) is witness.

Tulsidas sada Hari chera |
Keeje nath hridaye maha dera || 40 ||
Says Tulsi Das, who always remains Hari's servant'/
"Lord, make your home in my heart."

|| Doha ||

Pavan tanay sankat harana mangal murti roop |
Ram Lakhan Sita sahit hriday basau sur bhuup ||
Son of the Wind, destroyer of sorrow, embodiment of
blessings,
With Ram, Lakshman and Sita, LIVE IN MY HEART,
King of Gods!

|| Jai-Ghosh ||

Bol Bajarangabali ki jai
Pavan putra Hanuman ki jai
Jai Shri Ram

Seeyavara Ramchandra pada jai sharanam
Mangala moorati maaruta nandana
Sakala amangala moola nikandana
Refuge at the feet of Sita's lord, Ram.
You are the embodiment of blessings, Son of the Wind.
You destroy the root of everything that is inauspicious
and harmful.

ॐ

AARTEE SRI HANUMAN JI KI

Aarti Ki Jai Hanuman Lala Ki, Dushta Dalan Ragunath Kala Ki.
Ja Ke Bal Se Girivara Kaanpe, Rog Dosh Ja Ke Nikat Na Jhaanke.

Anjani Putra Mahabaldaye, Santan Ke Prabhu Sada Sahaye.
De Beeraha Raghunath Pathai, Lanka Jaari Siya Sudhi Laiye.

Lanka See Kot Samundra Se Khayi, Jaat Pavan Sut Baar Na Laiye.
Lanka Jaari Asur Sanhaare, Siya Ramji Ke Kaaj Sanvare.
Aarti Ki Jai Hanuman Lala Ki, Dushat Dalan Ragunath Kala Ki

Lakshman Moorchit Pade Sakare, Aani Sajeevana Pran Ubhaare.
Paith Pataala Tori Yamkare, Ahiravana Ke Bhuja Ukhaare.

Baayen Bhuja Asur Dal Mare, Daayen Bhuja Sab Santa Jana Tare.
Sura nara Muni Aarti Utare, Jai Jai Jai Hanuman Uchaare.

Kanchan Thaar Kapoor Lo Chhai, Aarti Karat Anjani Mai.
Jo Hanumanji Ki Aarti Gaave, Basi Baikuntha parampadh Pave.
Aarti Ki Jai Hanuman Lala Ki, Dushat Dalan Ragunath Kala Ki.

Lankaa vidhvansa kiye raghuraee, tulseedaasa prabhu keerati gaaee
Eti aarti bajaranga balee kee, aarti keeje hanuman lalla kee.

HANUMAN BHUJUN

Chale Hanuman Yaha Aye
Shree Ramji Ki Dhoon Machaye

Dhoon Machaye Aysi Dhoon Machaye
Chale Hanuman Yaha Aye
Shree Ramji Ki Dhoon Machaye
O Chale Hanuman, Come Over Here and Let's Chant Lord Ram's Name

Sitaram Naam Dhoon Aysi Machaye (2)
Sunker Aye Raghurai Shree Ramji Ki Dhoon Machaye

Chale Hanuman Yaha Aye
Shree Ramji Ki Dhoon Machaye
Chant Sitaram Naam in Such A Way That,
Shree Ram Comes When He Hears The Dhun

Bhakta Janoka Ghar Pawan Karva (2)
Avo Avo Ne Raghurai Shree Ramji Ki Dhoon Machaye
Chale Hanuman Yaha Aye
Shree Ramji Ki Dhoon Machaye
To Purify the Devotees' House (Hearts) Forever
Please Come Lord Ram (Raghuraay)

Gangaji Aye Jamnaji Aye (2)
Triveni Sangam Aye Shree Ramji Ki Dhoon Machaye
Chale Hanuman Yaha Aye
Shree Ramji Ki Dhoon Machaye
Gangaaji And Jamnaaji Comes (With Saraswati)
All the Three Auspicious Rivers Come Together

Das Janoki Yahi Vinanti (2)
Charan Kamal Balihari Shree Ramji Ki Dhoon Machaye
Chale Hanuman Yaha Aye
Shree Ramji Ki Dhoon Machaye
This Is the Servants' Request
We Bow and Surrender At Your Lotus Fee

PRATHANA

Abb somp diya iss jivan ka
Sab bhar toumahare hanthmei (2)

Hein jeet toumare hathon mein
Aur haar toumahare hanton mein)

Mera nishchay hai baas ek yahi
Ek baar toumhein pa jawoun mein (2)

Arpan kardou doonya bhar ja
Sab pyaar toumhare haton mein (2)

Jo jaag mein rahoun to aisse rahoun
Jiow jal mein kamal ka phool rahe (2)

Mera sab goon dosh samarpit ho
Kartar toumahe hanton mein (2)

Yadi manaw ka moujhe Janaam miley
To tawa charano ka pujari banou (2)

Iss pujyak ki ek ek rag ka
Ho taar tumhare haaton mein (2)

Jab jab sansar ka kaydi banoo
Nish kaam bhaw se karma karoo (2)

Phir anta samay mein praan tajoo
Nirakar toumhare hanton mein (2)

Moujh mein toujh mein bass bhed yahi

Mein naar toun Narayan hein (2)

Mein hou sansar ke hanton mein
Sansar toumaher haton mein (2)

MANTRAS

Kadli Garbha sambhoutam,
Karpuram tou pradirpitam
Arartikam aham kurvey,
Pasyaman vardo bhawa

Jayantee mangala Kali,
Bhadra Kali kapalini
Doorga sma Shiva dhatree,
Swaha swadha namoustoutey

Shatakaram bhujaga shyanaam,
Padmanabham suresham
Vishwa dharam Gagana sadrisham,
Megah varanam shubhan giam
Laxmi kanta kamal nayanam,
Yogir bidya nagamyam
Vandey Vishnu bhawa haram,
Sarva lokai kanatham

Vasoo devum sutam devam,
kansha chanoor mardanam
Devki parmananda,
Krisham vandey
Jagat gooroom

Hare Rama Hare Rama,
Rama Rama Hare Hare
Hare Krishna Hare Krishna,
Krishna Krishna   Hare Hare

Sarva mangal mangalyey,
Shivey sarvad sadhikey
Sharanyey trayambakey gowri,
Narayani namoustoutey

He rama purushotama narharee,
Narayanam keshawan
He Govind garurad dwaja guna nidhi,
Damo dara   madhavey
He Krishna kamalapatey
yadoopatey, Sita patey sripate
He vaikumthadi pate charachar pate,
Laxmi pate pahimam

Yada yada hi dharmashya,
Glaneer bhawatee Bharata
Abyoothanam adharmashya,
Tatat manam shrijamahayam

Paritranay sadhoonam,
Vinashaya cha dhouskritam
Dharma sans sthapnathaya,
 Sambhawamee yougey youge

Mangalam bhagwan Vishnu
Mangalam garourad dwaja
Mangalam poondaree kakcha
Mangalam tano haree

May auspiciousness be with Lord Vishnu,
may all auspiciousness be with the one who has Garuda
as his flag symbol.

~~~~~~~~

Avahanam na janamee
Najanamee visar Janam
Poojam chewa na janamee
Skyamtam parmeshwara

I know not how to invoke Thee
Nor the concluding rites of Puja
know not how to worship Thee
Please have mercy on me!

Mantra hinam kriyahinam
Bhaktee hinam janardhanam
Yatpoojitam maya devam
Paripoornam tadass Toomey

O Mother I know not Mantra
Nor the path of Action
Nor Devotion's way great
Be satisfied by my prayer!

~~~~~~~~~~~~

Papoham paap karmaham
Papatma paap sambhawa
Trahimam poondaree kaksha
Sarva papo haro haree

My egoism sinful, its work is sinful
Its soul is sinful, it is born of sin
Save me o God
Destroyer of all sins.

~~~~~~~~~~~~~

Poornamadaha poornamidam
Poornat poorna mou dachyatey
Poornashya poorna madaya
Poornamewa vashishyatey

*What is visible is the infinite. What is invisible is also
the infinite.*
Out of the Infinite Being the finite has come,
yet being infinite, only infinite remains.

~~~~~~~

Sarvey bhawantoo soukhina
Sarvey santoo niramaya
Sarvey bhadranee pashyantoo
Maa kaschit dhook bhag bhavet

Let all be happy, let all be healthy,
Let all see/experience auspiciousness,
Let no one be supressed/overwhelmed by grief.

~~~~~~~~~

Asato maa sat gamaya
Tamaso maa jyotir gamaya
Mritooyoma amritam gamaya
Lead me from darkness to light, Lead me from death to
immortality.

SHANTI PAATH

Twamewa mata cha pita twamewa,
Twemewa bandhu cha saka twamewa
Twemawa vidya dravinam twamewa,
Twamewa sharanam mama deva deva

You Truly are my mother, and You Truly are my father.
You Truly are my Relative and You Truly are my
Friend. You Truly are my knowledge, and You Truly
are my Wealth. You Truly are my All, My God of Gods.

Om dhior shanti
Ran Tarikshagwam
Shantih Pritvi
Shatihantih Raapah
Shantih Roshadhayah
Shantih Vanaspatayah
Shantih Vishwadewah
Shantih Bramhma
Shantih Sarvagwam
Shantih Shantireva
Shantih Shama
Shantih Redhi
Om Shantih Shantih Shantih.

This mantra is recited to attain universal peace....

Let peace be upon the immense sky that covers us and
the vast ethereal space that fills the universe,
Let peace rule over the entire earth, the water bodies
and all the forests with its trees, herbs and creepers,
Let peace be upon the endless universe that holds us,

*Let peace be upon the Divine Power that defines our
fates and the Brahma who led to our creation,
Let peace be upon every particle that forms a part of
this wide universe,
Om, bestow peace upon all beings, bestow peace upon
the world, bestow peace upon me.*

About the Author: Devina Ramchurn is a devout follower of Hinduism and a dedicated practitioner of its spiritual teachings. With a profound love for the tradition and a deep understanding of its essence, Devina has compiled this prayer book to offer a collection of sacred verses and chants for the spiritual nourishment of seekers.

Acknowledgments: We express our gratitude to the divine forces and spiritual guides whose grace and blessings have made this endeavour possible. We also extend our heartfelt thanks to all the saints, sages, and spiritual masters whose timeless wisdom continues to illuminate the path of our spiritual journey.

Publisher Information: Published by [Amazon] [London, UK.]

Disclaimer: While every effort has been made to ensure the accuracy and authenticity of the prayers and verses included in this book, readers are encouraged to consult with knowledgeable spiritual advisors or scholars for further guidance and interpretation. The author and publisher disclaim any liability or responsibility for any errors, omissions, or consequences arising from the use of the material contained herein.

Connect with Us: We value your feedback and welcome your inquiries. For questions, comments, or further information about our publications, please contact us at [dramchurn5@icloud.com].

ISBN: [ISBN 9798320937472]

Printed in: [Amazon]

Dedication: This book is dedicated to all seekers of truth and spiritual aspirants, may the divine grace guide and inspire your journey towards enlightenment and inner peace.

Om Shanti Shanti Shanti
(Peace, Peace, Peace)

Made in the USA
Columbia, SC
05 May 2024

35293602R00041